DESTINATION FREEDOM

FLYING OUT OF DEBT

VERONA GARLAND

ISBN 9798309668007

VERONA GARLAND

Publications, USA.

www.veronagarland.com

I joyously devote this book to:

ALEX and LEAH

who have taught me more, shown me more, and made me more than I could ever have imagined....

ACKNOWLEDGEMENT

I've had the honor of walking alongside Verona Garland as a friend and colleague and have witnessed, firsthand, her radiant spirit and unwavering dedication to shining a light on the path to prosperity. She doesn't merely speak about prosperity—she embodies it, living as a powerful example of what it means to align with abundance and step boldly into a life of limitless possibilities. With wisdom, compassion, and authenticity, she demystifies abundance and shows that prosperity isn't reserved for a select few—it is a birthright available to all who are willing to claim it. Her deep integrity, life experience and heartfelt care for others make this book a must-read for anyone ready to embrace abundance and discover freedom. This is more than a guide—it's a roadmap to create a life of true wealth—both internally and externally. Within these pages, you are invited to take off into the fullness of your life, guided by someone who genuinely wants to see you flourish.

-Amy Van Linge, Spiritual Director Unity Inspired Living

DESTINATION FREEDOM

FLYING OUT OF DEBT

INTRODUCTION

Welcome to your most fabulous, and presciently valuable journey! This journey has shown up right here and now because you are truly ready to brilliantly shine your light of prosperity. Yes, YOU!

You may have grabbed this book because you are feeling somewhat unlike a paragon of abundance or affluence. Or, you've decided the way out of this dilemma is educating yourself. Perhaps, you feel overwhelmed, mired in, or even completely overloaded with financial concerns.

My dearest reader, you've arrived upon the perfect vehicle for your transformation. This book will liberate, educate, and assist you in knowing your own prosperity, abundance , and sacred value. All that is required of you is a willingness to release your debt, consistent daily meditations, and a journal of your choice to chronicle your revelations, understandings, and progress. Let's have an agreement about meditation. This is the inner dialogue of your soul with the Creator of your Soul. It's been referred to as an “ inner shower”. As we cleanse our bodies regularly, we can cleanse our minds. Your meditation time is the gift you give to yourself each and every day. We’re not mandating a specific amount of time, styles of, or places of meditation. Your commitment is to a daily meditation practice. And, the regularity of your practice will outpicture in your Flying Out Of Debt experience.

Let’s fasten up and get going! It’s your time NOW! LET’S FASTEN UP!!

TABLE OF CONTENTS

1.	WHAT'S MY MONEY BEEN BEING?	11
2.	DECODING AND DETANGLING THE DEBT	26
3.	KNOWING THE KNOWING	44
4.	NAVIGATING THE FLOW OF ABUNDANCE	60
5.	JOINING THE EMBARKATION EXPRESS	72

CHAPTER ONE

WHAT'S MY MONEY BEEN BEING?

(FORGIVENESS & COMPASSION)

To begin, let's get clarity about debt.

FACT: DEBT IS NOT ABOUT THE MONEY! It's about identifying, extricating, and releasing beliefs, habits, and assumptions about one's self, while joyously re-seeding your affluence. It's been said that " money is the easiest thing to manifest".

Financial riches accompany a grounded

consciousness in Source and Supply from within. The Life Force chooses, in fact It desires plentitude as our inherent existence. YES, IT'S TRUE!! We come to the planet coded in affluence- the flow of prosperous abundance!

You see, I've taken this exact same journey in the course my life. As an International Flight Attendant and Purser, I have shopped the world.

What else made travel scintillating besides shopping? Every country awaited, overflowing with commodities that were a must to bring home. And, of course, this spending fever continued when I returned to my home base.

The ensuing credit card debt shadowed me for many years. I was paying the minimum while accumulating even more debt. That is, until I reached, for my financial stamina, the point of no return. I was $35K in credit card debt to various department stores and the Visa Corporation. I was going to work to pay credit card debts. I felt weighed down, disliked myself, and truly helpless.

I wasn't alone in this predicament as I learned that most Americans are between $8K-100k in debt.

However, sleepless nights, and stress-filled and tearful days brought me to my tipping point.

So, I turned within, decided to surrender the recriminations fueling my self destruction, hunkered down in my spiritual practices, and prepared to be the best and highest debt free affluent version of Me!

This took some seriously radical self insights, and mostly a persevering desire to be FREE!

I want you to know that this felt like standing in a 3 way mirror in my original birthday suit on top

of the Tour Eiffel, Great Wall of China, and the Sydney Opera House all at once. Yes, these were places I'd reveled in visiting. Yet, lots of the opinions, ideas, and reactions of the group thinking hastened deluges of my teary outbursts as I attempted to carry on my life as a wife, mother, and conscientious flight attendant.

So, where did I begin? What created the stopgap to get things shifting? What really was my money being?

Spirituality has led my existence since I can remember being me. My life's quest is completely interwoven in the Divine. And, so I turned within to meditation, prayer, and contemplation. The very first answer that blazed into my consciousness was the principle of : FORGIVENESS

I was being given permission to forgive

all- my behaviours, my credit card providers, and my self imposed condemnations. Could it be this easy? Had I unearthed the secret actions ? Yes and YES! When I decided to enter the present moments, the floodgates of abundant prosperity were given their clearance to fling themselves open!

Let's unravel forgiveness. We hear lots about forgiveness in all facets of living. Yet, it may feel foreign or unapproachable. Actually, forgiveness is

known for unblocking the FLOW of all

activity. It's the SuperPower of Prospering! And, forgiveness IS NOT forgetting or giving a pass to situations or people.

So, how does it work? Where to start? What's next?

Here are Practical Forgiveness Tips:

- BE CIRCUMSPECT WITH YOUR THOUGHTS
  - Firstly, let's begin within. What are you thinking about yourself? Does that carry over to others?
- BE RADICALLY SCRUPULOUS

WITH YOUR WORDS

  - What are you saying to yourself and others?

    Is your inner dialogue really

    representative of what you believe?

- TAKE BABY STEPS
  - In your every activity, gather up

    baby steps of awareness. Perhaps

    give yourself the morning to be

    acutely alert.

- FORGIVE AND SURRENDER ALL
  - As events, people, and happenings

    bubble up

- FORGIVE IN LOVE
  - Give yourself permission to revisit

any seeming wrongs in order to forgive them Imagine a golden cord of connection being cut with the scissors of love, disconnecting you from any past occurrences. You can now take dominion of your existence, from this very moment forward! What a n exhilarating feeling! And, in case you're wondering about the resolution of those who you may feel have wronged you, rest assured that the blessings of perfect order are continuously at work. If you dissect the word, it spells:

for-give. This means that we get to embody the givingness of compassion as we exemplify surrendering the past. And, it's of utmost importance to keep yourself safe and secure from any such further behaviour or interactions.

Practice these habits at your workplace, in traffic, while grocery shopping, or in your family interactions. Let them merge effortlessly together. You get the idea- be cognizant. And when/if unforgiveness shows up, deluge it with the fascinating and magnetic elixir of COMPASSION.

So, what is compassion, how does it work?

And it helps me in what ways?

Compassion is the flip side of the coin of judgement. Judging one another can spread like a prairie fire when given favorable ingredients- comparison, competition, and unforgiveness. Yet, allowing yourself to take the inner perspective of the one being judged douses the flames with understanding and empathy.

Where this flip can be the most challenging is with ourselves. Some of the most unforgiving thoughts, some old thinking morphed into belief systems can be lodged in the crevices of our own mind. By accepting these cues from the mind, we not only create false truths, we absorb these distortions. Then, these falsehoods can appear as our personal system of principles.

True compassion is the flowing, tender, impenetrable adhesive of Love- love of Self, love in the oneness of all Beings, and love simply for the lovingness extended unconditionally to each of us by Spirit. Compassion is YOU!

And, how did I start? I forgave myself the seeming insurmountable mountain of debt. I utilized metaphysical meditations, I accepted the brilliance of the Divine that I am, and I admitted that I had done the very best with the information that I had at the time. I faced the debt head on, with compassion leading the way. And, I compiled the entire amount: infusing each amount with as much forgiveness as I could muster.

In the beginning, it was an activity of "

being willing to be willing" to forgive compassionately. Mostly, in my forgiveness journey, I committed to remaining present in the now. My vehicle of transformation has pushed away from the blocks (an airplane's beginning detachment from it's previous position on the ground), my willingness muscle is firing up, and my sojourn of liberation has begun! Are you coming along?

CHAPTER TWO

DETANGLING & DECODING THE DEBT

ACCEPTANCE and APPROVAL

When you pass a mirror or plate glass window, gazing at yourself, what do you see? Or do you even take the time to admire the spectacular specimen of goodness, brilliance, and fabulousness that is You? Are you an estate sale hidden from yourself? Is there a critical parent or teacher, from the past, creating the inner dialogue about you?

Does it occur to you to truly acknowledge the magnificence of the Universe that is you? Are you aware that you " are made in the image and likeness of the Divine, the Life Force, the Allness of the Universe"? Does it ever occur to you that

you are a bespoke miracle? Or, are you " hiding your light under a bushel"? Perhaps, the programming of not being braggadocious has been dampening your vigor. Or, your inborn radiance has been held down for seeming rightful reasons.

In my life I had somehow scrambled up these sacred truths. I knew that style, artistry, brilliance, joy, verve and beauty truly lived within me. From my girlhood, these God qualities made themselves apparent to me. However, there was that part of me that thought these attributes were odd and/or different. The life of integration, assimilating, and vigorous goal achieving that was mine overflowed with the clarification of my differentness. I was regularly "the only" in my every activity. While this way of life brought forth myriad habits of strength, fortitude, steadfastness, perseverance, and bravery, it also reaped a harvest of my wearing an invisibility cloak over my God given qualities. The qualities of openness, vulnerability, tenderness, and welcoming weren't at the forefront of my regular endeavours. By going within, to the presence of Spirit that was the incineration of my light, I realized that my existence was missing the real truth of my purposes for being on this planet, at this time. With immense surprise and clarity, I

realized that by not putting myself and my

skills and talents at the forefront, I was darkening the zeal, verve, spirituality, imagination,exuberance, vivaciousness, and effervescence that I AM.

With great faith and trust, I decided to emancipate myself from my self imposed shrinkage and obscurity. I began affirming the Truths of myself- I am strong, brave, effervescent, patient, greatness, love, joy, glee, goodness, at peace with myself, etc. I affirmed each and every wondrousness that popped into my heart. Then, I followed the brain in my heart's clearness with great expectation. Whenever the old beliefs or

ideas crept up, I gave thanks for the excavation blessing them on their way! It became a fun game of acceptance as well as approval. And, it meshed quite easily with my increased practices of forgiveness and compassion. It felt as if I was constructing a sacred, customized garment of love, accomplishment, joy, and receptivity.

And now in these revealing moments, away we go! Doesn't it feel great to have what I call some practicalities? Your internal GPS-God Positioning System is always working for your highest and best good. We've buckled up with forgiveness and compassion. Let's get the wheels off the ground!!

I invite you to create an advertisement or social media post about yourself. This is for the purposes of your learning and growth here, only. No need to actually post, unless it gets you in the groove of acceptance and approval! However, I invite you to price this advert about YOU! What are the qualities you admire about yourself? What are your gifts? In what ways do you automatically excel?

What is yours to bless and share with the planet? In what ways do you participate in the vast richness from within? Reflecting upon yourself right now, what do you appreciate, admire, and thoroughly get a thrill from? What actions have you taken that you feel good about, and what custom qualities of YOU did these utilize? Once again, you get the idea. Have some fun with these questions, place them in your sacred journal, and reflect upon them at day's end each evening. Be sure to clearly and succinctly answer these questions. When other thoughts creep in, once again, bless them on their way in compassion and love. A wonderful affirmation for these moments is: CLEAR, CANCEL, SURRENDER.

And, please be gentle with yourself as such thoughts of opposition pop up quite often. The part of us that's comfy with the previous, old ways of speaking to yourself is having a most difficult time, in no longer being the leader. You see, there's a part of us that can be referred to as the ego. The most common of the ego may be connected with self aggrandizement. Perhaps, we've heard someone called an "egomaniac" because they speak incessantly about themselves. For our purposes, I refer to the ego as that part of one's being that keeps you safe in a crosswalk- don't walk on the red. Or the ego instructions that remind you to drive defensively on a busy freeway during rush hour. However, some ego behaviour can "edge God out". It's the statements that advise" don't try that, what if it's dangerous?" or " what makes you think you can do that?" or even " what if it fails?" etc. In these instances, the ego is valiantly trying to keep it's position as " the brains of this operation". Nevertheless, there's our Inner Voice. Remember the spiritual GPS we discussed earlier? Our Divine Self creates and unfolds, in safety, and guidance, our highest, wisest, and most grace-filled next steps. Let's not forget that the Life Force can only bring It's gifts and blessings through/as each one of us. Yes, not only are you the Vessel, you are the Elucidation of Universal Allness!

In setting your tone, I invite you to play music that makes your heart sing ; give yourself space wafting with smells that please your olfactory senses, and plunge into these further questions with vigor! Think of answering these questions about your bestie, BFF, or "your girl". You need not make this an overly planned activity. Merely do it to the intensity of your desire to fly out of debt. Are you ready for your next exhilarating, revealing, and healing layover??

Here are a few nudges from my own experience into this adventure of truth. I set the tone with music- each time a different genre- classical, show tunes, gospel, pop, anything that reflected my pureness of acceptance and approval. And, yes, this marvelous movement can be repeated regularly. Next, I set the olfactory tone with ylang ylang, lavender, citrus scents in candles, room diffusers, even perfumes sprayed on my warm spots of my body temple. Finally, I chose the most comfy place in my home- a plump arm chair occupying an eastward facing space in my bedroom.

These are merely beginning suggestions. I invite you to breathe in your customized environment reflecting your spectacular Self!

WHO ARE YOU? TRULY, DEEP WITHIN, WHO ARE YOU?

Do all of your titles, descriptions, degrees,

or differentiations make you who you are? It's a fact that the composite truth of you is encoded within every atom and fiber of your being. I believe the more important question is, whose are you? Did you know that you belong in the Cosmic Crown of the Universe? You are a one of a kind gem in the mystic container of Oneness.

We arrive on the planet packed full to the brim, overflowing with the lavish richness of the Universe imprinted into our being. To the delight of Source Energy, we each incarnate exactly in/on time. The Creator requires an instrument for It's expression, unfoldment, and embodiment, abundance, and givingness.

YOU ARE THAT VESSEL!

Our abundance is ancient, eternal, and pre-destined to perfection. You are the fulfillment of source and supply flowing as the fluidity of the Divine. Once again, YOU ARE THE VESSEL

NOW, TAKE A DEEP BREATH,

TAKE IT IN, LET IT FLOW OUT…

WHO ARE YOU? READY FOR A LOVE RELATIONSHIP?

Our debt can be a direct representation of losing our way in self approval, self acceptance, and self remembrance resulting in unforgiveness. Isn't it amazing how this all hooks together? One heals the other, and the prosperity flows.

CHAPTER THREE

KNOWING THE

KNOWING THE SHIFT APPEARS

GRATITUDE

You may be thinking, what could I have to be grateful for? My finances appear to be in shambles, each month brings more stress, and what kind of person am I? If you've truly begun the adventure in the two previous chapters, you're probably ready for the Big Reveal! What brings the prosperity shift? When does the "floodgate flinging open" whoosh forward? Where's the supreme secret of indebtedness?

Affluence is defined as" being in the flow". Thus far, we've embraced being forgiving, compassionate, accepting, and approving. All of these movements are " in the flow" of universal givingness. Can you feel the differences in your feeling tone, your stress levels, or your general well being? It's been said, "It isn't where you've come from , it's where you are going" Ella Fitzgerald

Being grateful can be where you are going. It's your ultimate choice. Being gratitude activates and accelerates the Universal Law of Source and Supply. Being gratitude is pre-ordering your heart's desires unfolding as YOU!

This tenet may feel the most dichotomous. Can I be thankful for the state my finances are in, this very moment? Is this a magic trick? MOST DEFINITELY, IT IS NOT! When we are grateful, the vibration of our being shifts and changes. It's an energetic wanting to magnetize Itself to each and every one of our cells, atoms, fibers, and so much more. Embodying this energetic, brings us into direct harmony with the Cosmic Systems of Circulation. We have the opportunity to ensconce ourselves into perspective shift, being grateful for what has the nerve to appear wrapped in scratchy, plain sandpaper versus silky wrapping of the palest blue tied with a satiny white ribbon. What sort of incongruous silliness is happening? And, in what ways do I translate these happenings?

We get to be appreciative of everything, even the seemingly discordant happenings by curling ourselves completely up in the Vibration of Gratitude. And, this begins with a perspective shift. By accepting that in the midst of it all, the goodness of the Universe is discovering Itself as YOU, the shift radiates from your every thought, emotion, and belief. It may begin with small steps of trust, and before you know it, KAPOW, you are in the Flow of Richness!

Remember learning to ride a bike, read a book, play an instrument, or even brush your teeth? This is the very same vibration of trust, expectancy, and growth. And, the twist is the ability to shift our preconceived ideas about every single action, interaction, and happening. This simply requires stepping away from the past, remaining in the now. You've already begun cultivating this skill in Forgiveness and Compassion. Gratitude propels you into this very moment, while simultaneously dissolving all fear.

Since fear is truly “ false evidence appearing real”, then what’s to say that there aren't a myriad of ways to discern each and every happening? Can you allow yourself to feel the ubiquitous transference? Let’s call it “Getting A Grip On My Attitude”! What does it take? Am I equipped?

What’s the timeline?

Firstly, this transformation takes ruthless excavation of any fears or stubborn ungratefulness. By this I mean going within, asking what wants to be known, owning your attachment to these beliefs, and willingness to surrender. This can be accomplished in daily meditation, contemplation, and introspection. It is imperative that you continue your commitment of spending time in solitude, stillness, and silence.

This listening space is sacredly productive. Remember, it's the gift of the Universe giving of Itself through and as YOU!

As these past ideas and beliefs come

forward, you get to do exactly what we've suggested earlier: bless these entities with love, surrender, and permission to move onward to another energetic. Here's where your creative Self has an opportunity to blaze into this transformation. You can flip the script on those past beliefs with affirmations. An affirmation is the mental equivalent of what your heart desires. The desires of your heart are the Life Force wanting to bring Itself forth as YOU!

Let's say your past belief is " My debt is

going to trail me throughout my life". The more you think, speak, believe this statement, the more it grows within your existence. Your " flip the script " affirmation could be " The movement of indebtedness in my life activates imagination, abundance, and my oneness in prosperity." See how it works?The important part of affirmations is the feeling tone. Remember as a child how as you wrote your Christmas list, you already felt happy to receive your requested gift? Close your eyes , right now, go within, and feel the grateful anticipation. Get the idea? This is the feeling tone of affirmations- knowing that the demonstration of this statement is already gestating, growing and bursting upon the scene.

In my own indebtedness, gratitude was my next step. It's a well known principle that Gratitude is an activator of Abundance. So, what brings gratitude? Is it things, gifts, occurrences? I believe that Gratitude is birthed in Faith. Faith can be seen as: "feeling aware in trust & happiness". Faith germinates in trusting unseen reality. Faith is the spiritual mechanism for taking leaps in life. And this same faith is a catalyst of gratitude.

In my debt free adventure, I realized that I was being given gratitude for the understanding of exactly where I was in my life in the present moment. I was given the opportunity to actually deal with the debt. Previously, I wasn't very taken with myself. My self forgiveness quotient had been quite low. Up until this time, I was playing tapes of criticism, perfectionism, and doubt in those inner conversations. As I forgave myself with the utmost compassion, I was given the safety of viewing this surrendering of any judgment as my pathway forward. Distinctly, in moments of stillness and solitude, I could feel the journey of indebtedness loosing itself up. And in giving thanks for what I'd previously termed " a terrible circumstance", I surrendered all that was blocking my innate prosperous life. I had arrived at the juncture of change, gratitude, and excited expectancy- financial freedom. It's often driven by impulse buying in the absence of forgiveness, compassion, self acceptance and self approval.

Allowing ourselves to accept the divinely perfect order of our abundant life gives faith and gratitude the spaciousness of growth, expansion, and prosperity.

So, here's our fun and flow in the practicalities of indebtedness release: Give thanks for every single happening, thing, or experience. Remember to recognize the kernels of goodness in everything, even the items that may feel yucky, obstructive, and even adverse. It's there, awaiting your discoveries.

Wrap your debts in a blanket of loving appreciation. Look at all they're revealing about your highest and greatest expansiveness as you.

Affirm the experiential growth of abundant prosperity within/as you. In these statements, allow the feeling tone of your greatest desires to lead the way.

So, we've arrived at cruise. Can you feel the splendor, understanding, and possibilities of an abundant, prosperous, plentiful YOU? And, as we give thanks, the knowing of abundance pours Itself through, around, and as us. When the human appearances in my affairs are different, I know that my attitude of gratitude opens all doorways to affluence, wealth, and peace of mind.

CHAPTER FOUR

NAVIGATING THE FLOW OF ABUNDANCE (VISION and FOCUS)

Have you ever encountered Baccarat crystal? It's known for the artistry and craftsmanship involved in each piece, no matter how big or small. The Baccarat company standards are the highest possible in crystal creation. These pieces are exceptionally crafted by well trained and experienced artisans, using traditional techniques. Most decidedly, the pieces are renowned for their clarity and brilliance.

You're probably thinking, what might this have to do with my destination of freedom from indebtedness? Well, here's the connection, to navigate the flow of abundance within and as you, it's imperative to embody, embrace, and express VISION and FOCUS. Just as the artisans of each and every Baccarat piece of crystal art enfold the clarity of the finished product well before the end is accomplished. The craftsperson has the clarity of vision and focus before any glass is blown or cut.

The creation of each of us, by the Creator embodies this same unequivocal attention. You are a supreme work of the Life Force's artistry. Divine craftspersonship has brought you forth here and now. You are a one of a kind wonder. And, guess what? This creative geniusness wants only the boundless richness, limitless opulence, and immeasurable givingness for YOU!

The journey of Flying out of Debt requires the exact same polestar, the identical devoir from within YOU. Are you ready to accept and realize that it's already here? You came to the planet already encoded. Aaaah, breathe that in for a moment, let it reside in your completeness…

As I navigated my own Flying out of Debt adventure, I initially chose to clarify my focus. What was my money being/doing for me? What did I want from my financial outlay? And, where were my financial values?

First, I also decided to cease my love/hate relationship with money, credit cards and debt. I realized that debt is the greatest acceptance of confidence for my expressing the lavish abundance of the Universe wanting to emerge as ME. Yes, those to whom I may be indebted are showing resoluteness in my ability to repay. We're in a believing boogie together! Doesn't this feel fantastic? What a shift, huh?

Secondly, I decided on my financial values. I want my riches to do good in this world, enrich others lives, and move it forward in splendiferous ways. I came to understand that as I repaid my debts, I was circulating in loving generosity.

Thirdly, from my financial outlay, I desired peace, comfort, and joy. It became incumbent upon me to give exponentially of these exact qualities to get them back. It's a well known ancient wisdom fact, that in order to have something, you must be willing to give it away. I embarked on countless expeditions of being the ultimate giver of these qualities.

Along the way, I chose to learn and emulate the differentiation of purposeful debt versus mindless debt. For me , purposeful debt aligns with my financial values, choices, and circulations. I discovered examples of purposeful debt such as mortgage, food, and fuel. On the other hand, mindless debt veered away from my core principles and beliefs. In my experiences, it was often driven by impulse buying in the absence of forgiveness, compassion, self acceptance and self approval. Mass media marketing exacerbated my self imposed feelings of unworthiness.

One of my best examples is purchasing designer shoes, of the same style, in several colors. No, I hadn't any idea where I was going to wear these items, or even when. I simply collected them. This was iametrically opposed to my values, principles, and vision of my monies. Do you feel the differences? Can you sense the digression from a dedicated financial plan? And, does purposeful or non-purposeful come to mind?

The Universe can only give you that about which you are completely clear. Imagine going shopping for your ultimate gift with no spending limits, in focus, clarity, and vision. How does that feel in your soul, mind, and body? Then, imagine taking the same shopping trip with sketchy ideas, no specifications, and fuzzy ideas about your desires. What a bizarre, baffling, and disconcerting experience this would be. Do you get the difference? Source and Supply awaits our spoken word- from our hearts, minds, and our lips as well as clarity, focus, and a steadfast visioning practice to activate our innate riches. Muddied requests fall into the category of indefinable asks.

Are you excited about the practical actions of this juncture in the journey? You've done splendid works! They're all bound to one another. And, you hold the key of unlocking. Let's aviate to the next level.

Be aware of your own affair with your monies. Accept that a new path is being taken, wrapped in safety, sanctuary, tenderness, and loving kindness. Understand purposeful debt and mindless debt. Bless them both , while remaining concentrated on your circulation behaviours. Hold your financial values foremost in all transactions.

Repay your debts, joyously, sweetly, celebratorily, and lovingly. Make your payments in the ways you want to receive the riches, wealth, and abundance of the Universe. As you press send on virtual payments, give compassion. If you pay by checks, deliver bliss along with your missive. If electronic payments on your phone are your utmost convenience. As you point your phone, convey love in your clicking.

In the stillness of meditative thought, visioning , and focus be ready to open to the distinct Riches wanting to be given as/for/to you. Be ready to receive!

CHAPTER FIVE

JOINING THE EMBARKATION EXPRESS (PRACTICAL EXPANSIONS)

We've been on quite the flight together! From forgiveness/compassion, to acceptance/ approval, to gratitude, to vision/ focus, the spectacular flight out of debt has taken form and taken off. In my flying days, the thrill of takeoff always amazed and energized me. Here I was embarking upon a fresh, vibrant, all possibilities journey. And as I began my own bespoke Flying Out Of Debt undertaking, I could sense and feel myriad possibilities. And as such, your bespoke adventure can only be propelled by your steadfast desire, work ethic, and transparency with the Universe.

Our time, in these pages, can be fruitful, comforting , and plentiful. The choice is yours to take dominion over your wealth, abundance, and innate prosperity. The Universe wants to express and give of Itself in/as YOU! Usually, embarkation requires some sort of documentation, identification, and confirmation of one's intention. We have exactly our own version of embarkation , as we arrive at DESTINATION FREEDOM!

Let's begin with Expectancy. Expectancy can sometimes lead to utter falsehoods. In our world, there may be a belief in balancing out abundances.

By that I mean, that we may have been quite insidiously taught an all pervasive belief in " not enough ness". These two ideas generally come together in the end result of believing that if I get my most desired outcome, someone else is being deprived, in some way. This probably feels familiar somewhere deep inside of you. How could there be more than enough to have AND to share? Infinite giving is the unrivaled law of nature. When a drop of dew dries, is there not another the following morning? Even, sometimes, the fluid naturalness of acceptance can become it's own stumbling block. Who wants abundant riches if it deprives another? This familiar refrain impedes our acceptance of that which is our original birthright. However, expectancy speeds progress, gestates the infinite flow of Source and Supply.

And, yet, the Universe continuously finds a container for It's most sumptuous appearances on the planet. Remember, YOU are the vessel of infinite goodness! Expect the most opulent, lavish, sumptuous riches as yours!

In my expectancy, I get to decide the ways in which this unlocks the gates of all possibility. As I allow myself to stretch beyond any previous experiences, I can completely unhinge the prosperity gates to receive abundant supply in myriad ways.

So, taking the "Embarkation Leap' is truly a state of mindful expectation. What good awaits my approach, even in ways unanticipated by me? Are you up for this bounce, plunge, and arrival into FREEDOM?

In steadfast expectancy, we begin by

chronicling each and every debt. This includes purposeful and mindless ones. Yes, I know it may feel scary, and you are not alone. Remember the Life Force's desire is for you to prosper. And you are one with that which has created you. Starting your own fresh journal to list these promises and confidences begins the documentation and identification part of this journey. Here's where you get to use some Spiritual Technology, along with practical financial practices. With the exercise of Golden Goals, outlined in the Edwene Gaines book, The Four Spiritual

Laws of Prosperity, you set a specific date for the repayment of each debt. Remember, purposeful debts- mortgage, food, fuel, etc, aren't required to be included. Daily and nightly affirming: "I accept, I receive, and I claim dissolution of debt by ____ your chosen dates. These goals were a list of 12 Golden Goals. Please allow yourself to be realistic as well as expectant. As we've previously discovered, expectancy activates the fluidity and flexibility of abundance. You are sending distinct messages to the Universal Flow. If you unrealistically send a message to Universal

Law, your insincerity rings through as your most distinctive request. Along with this Golden Goal Practice, I suggest you make a spreadsheet for each debt, it's due date monthly, and payment. The important bonus is that each month you repay MORE than the minimum. Trust me, as you Forgive Compassionately, Accept and Approve of yourself and others, holding all happenings in Gratitude, while embracing Vision and Focus, the abundance will flow. What's of utmost importance is that your every thought, action, and endeavor overflows with kindness, gentleness, and tenderness towards yourself.

Imagine the infant You. How would you treat, speak to, hold her/his/their desires? The Creator of the Universe truly adores You, delights in You, and is tickled to life with your existence. Can you allow yourself to emulate and express the same about/for yourself?

Your spectacular habits of Meditation, Visioning, and Affirmations now get to take their first class seats in your life. Yes, these are your newly regular guiding flood lights of abundance, opulence, plentitude, prosperity, and more in any circumstance of debt/plenty. They are both the same in the Life Force.

You'd probably like to know how/if/when these behaviours played out in my life. Well, I spreadsheeted each debt with its specifics, while simultaneously claiming and naming my Golden Goals each morning and every night. As the debt receded, I added more to my list of 12.

Each debt got paid more than its minimum amount, if even $1 dollar more.

Before, I slipped into the “ doing” I chose to vision, focus, and articulate my financial values, as we did in Chapter Four- Vision and Focus. This was daily accompanied by Gratitude- for any confusion or understanding within me, for the ability to return/repay to those who had entrusted with me my circulation of abundance.

Affirmations of abundance, self-love, self-acceptance, self-approval, compassion, and forgiveness filled every space in my home- each room, my auto, my work suitcase, my gym bag, and each purse (remember I was a shopper who purchased in multiples- LOL) , every piece/part of my life!! Affirmations accompanied my trips to many different countries, becoming the interior designs of my hotel rooms. With patches of darkness, impatience, pain, and confusion I grew through it all. My perspective shifts were the harbingers of my upcoming freedom. As I stretched away from old beliefs, new knowledge filled the vacuum. Quick hits of awareness balanced out any dips into murkiness.

And 18 months later, I emerged credit card debt free. The Universe sent unexpected abundance in the forms of class action suit payments, unexpected gifts from family members, and debts showing zero balance inexplicably. Along with these seeming miracles, I changed. I came back into the purity, abundance, clarity, awareness, and embrace of the Divine Truth that I AM.

You, my dearest, are ready because you are holding this book in your hands- physically or virtually. Your embarkation into FREEDOM awaits!

ABOUT THE AUTHOR

Reverend Verona Garland is a transformational spiritual leader, teacher, and prosperity mentor dedicated to helping individuals unlock their highest potential.

Before stepping into ministry, Reverend Verona spent over 40 years as an International Purser for a major international carrier, flying primarily throughout Asia. This experience deepened her global perspective, cultural awareness, and ability to connect with people from all walks of life—insights she now brings into her spiritual teachings and prosperity work.

As the former Assistant Minister of Agape Bay Area in Oakland, CA (2017-2024), an affiliate center of Agape International in Los Angeles, she carried forward the mission of spiritual awakening, empowerment, and abundance for all. She is now affiliated with CSL Kenya (cslkenya.org), where she serves on the Board of Trustees and was a featured presenter at the 2024 *Heart of Africa* Conference in Nairobi.

With deep roots in Interfaith teachings and New Thought principles, Reverend Verona is an ordained Interfaith minister through the Emerson Theological Institute and a Centers for Spiritual Living minister. These credentials, combined with her life experience and unwavering commitment to truth, make her a sought-after speaker, counselor, and mentor for those seeking both spiritual and financial transformation.

Reverend Verona's gift lies not only in her ability to inspire but also in her practical and actionable approach to personal and financial growth. She doesn't just speak about prosperity—she embodies it. Through her work, she has empowered countless individuals to shift their perspectives, move beyond limiting beliefs, and align with the limitless possibilities available to them.

Her teachings emphasize that prosperity is

not reserved for a select few—it is the birthright of all. Whether addressing spiritual seekers, entrepreneurs, professionals, or those struggling with financial hardship, her message is the same: abundance is available to you, but you must be willing to claim it.

At the heart of Reverend Verona's work is her newest ministry, Prosperity On The Move—a transformative initiative that serves all who are committed to identifying, understanding, and manifesting their own prosperity.

This ministry goes beyond financial literacy; it is a soulful journey into abundance consciousness, designed to help individuals heal their relationship with money, shift limiting beliefs, and cultivate financial well-being from the inside out.

Reverend Verona Garland believes that each person has a divine inheritance of prosperity, love, joy, and success. Her work is an invitation—to step out of fear, to move beyond doubt, and to claim the rich, abundant, and meaningful life that is waiting.

For those ready to soar into a new reality, Reverend Verona stands as a guide, mentor, and cheerleader, reminding us all that true freedom—spiritually, financially, and emotionally—is not only possible but inevitable when we embrace who we truly are.

For more information about

Reverend Verona Garland,

visit **www.veronagarland.com**

www.ingramcontent.com/pod-product-compliance
Lightning Source LLC
LaVergne TN
LVHW050922210926
848482LV00012B/501